Keto Crock Pot Cookbook for Beginners

50 No-Fuss And Low Fat Recipes For Beginners. Eat Amazing Food, Lose Weight Fast, Increase Your Energy Level And Boost Health In A Few Steps

Clara Smith

Table of Contents

Introduction

The crockpot has long been a favorite kitchen implement for the 'set-it-and-forget-it' meal. It's a wonderful invention by whoever thought it up, and it has saved many a few dollars on electricity by not needing to keep the stove and oven on for extended hours and all day. So, what really is a crockpot?

A crockpot is also called a slow cooker or a casserole crockpot. These nicknames refer to the same kitchen appliance, and it is one of the most used reheating methods today. It is basically a cooker with a glazed ceramic bowl that has a tight sealing lid. It is because of the liquid that will go in with the food. The crockpot is then plugged into an electrical socket in the kitchen for it to work.

The crockpot slow cooking method involves basically depositing the ingredients you desire to cook into the crockpot bowl (usually by stirring it with a wooden spoon or a ladle), adding the liquid of choice, cooking it for a few hours until it's done. These used to be the standard cooking methods in kitchens, and they have stayed the same with the invention of the crockpot. Nowadays, most crockpots have interiors thermostatically controlled to ensure that it's set at the right temperature during the cooking process to not over-cook your meals.

The best in crockpot slow cooking is finding that low and slow recipe. Recipes that are low in time length are usually very low in steps, and not much work is involved. It usually leads to the much sought after 'set it and forget it' kind of meal. Imagine not having to watch your meals cook slowly as you work on other tasks; you can avoid the temptation of peeking or checking on it too often and not having to worry about burning or crusting on the sides of your crockpot. When cooking at low heat, you don't have to worry about your meal exploding all over the kitchen or all the grease falling out and sticking to the bottom of your crock.

CHAPTER 1:

Breakfast

1.   Sausage-Stuffed Eggplants

Preparation time: 10 minutes

Cooking time: 6 hours

Servings: 6

Ingredients:

- 12 ounces sausage links, chopped

- 2 cloves of garlic, minced

- 2 tablespoons rosemary, fresh

- Salt and pepper to taste

- 3 small eggplants, sliced

- 6 slices mozzarella cheese

Directions:

1. Mix all ingredients in a bowl. Place in a Ziploc bag and write the date when the recipe is made. Place inside the freezer.

2. Once you are ready to cook the meal, allow to thaw on the countertop for at least 2 hours. Line the bottom of the crockpot with foil. Grease with cooking spray.

3. Pour into the crockpot and cook on low for 6 hours or on high for 4 hours.

Nutrition:

Calories: 471

Carbohydrates: 6.3g

Protein: 16.83g

Fat: 38.9g

2. Zucchini Sausage Breakfast "Bake"

Preparation time: 5 minutes

Cooking time: 4 hours

Servings: 12

Ingredients:

- 1-pound Italian sausages, chopped

- ½ cup coconut flour

- 2 teaspoons baking powder

- 1 teaspoon salt

- ½ teaspoon pepper

- 8 ounces cream cheese

- 10 large eggs

- 2 small zucchinis, grated and excess water squeezed

- 4 cloves of garlic, minced

- 1 cup cheese, shredded

Directions:

1. Mix all ingredients in a bowl. Place in a Ziploc bag and write the date when the recipe is made. Place inside the freezer.

2. Once you are ready to cook the meal, allow to thaw on the countertop for at least 2 hours. Pour into the crockpot. Close the lid and cook on high for 3 hours or on low for 4 hours.

Nutrition:

Calories: 344

Carbohydrates: 6.3g

Protein: 21g

Fat: 27g

3.   Cheddar Jalapeno Breakfast Sausages

Preparation time: 5 minutes

Cooking time: 6 hours

Servings: 12

Ingredients:

- 12 medium-sized breakfast sausages

- 1 jalapeno pepper, chopped

- ½ cup cheddar cheese, grated

- ¼ cup heavy cream

- Salt and pepper to taste

Directions:

1. Mix all ingredients in a bowl. Place in a Ziploc bag and write the date when the recipe is made. Place inside the freezer.

2. Once you are ready to cook the meal, allow to thaw on the countertop for at least 2 hours. Pour into the crockpot.

3. Close the lid and cook on low for 6 hours or on high for 4 hours. Garnish with parsley on top.

Nutrition:

Calories: 472

Carbohydrates: 1.2g

Protein: 32.6g

Fat: 42.4g

4.　　Chocolate Peanut Butter Breakfast Bars

Preparation time: 15 minutes

Cooking time: 6 hours

Servings: 12

Ingredients:

- 4 ounces cream cheese, softened

- 1 large egg, beaten

- 2 cups almond flour

- ½ cup chunky peanut butter

- ½ cup heavy cream

- 3 tablespoons stevia sweetener

- 1 teaspoon vanilla extract

- ½ cup dark chocolate chips

Directions:

1. In a large mixing bowl, mix together the cream cheese, egg, almond flour, peanut butter, heavy cream, stevia, vanilla extract, and chocolate chips. Use a hand mixer to combine everything.

2. Place in a Ziploc bag and write the date when the recipe is made. Place inside the freezer. Once you are ready to cook the meal, allow to thaw on the countertop for at least 2 hours.

3. Line the bottom of the crockpot with foil and grease with cooking spray. Pour the batter into the crockpot. Close the lid and allow to cook for 5 hours or on low or 3 hours on high.

Nutrition:

Calories: 170

Carbohydrates: 4.4g

Protein: 8.1g

Fat: 20.5g

5.   Breakfast Sausage and Peppers

Preparation time: 10 minutes

Cooking time: 6 hours

Servings: 5

Ingredients:

- 1-pound Italian sausages, minced

- ½ head of cauliflower, grated

- 1 small tomato paste

- 1 small onion, diced

- ½ head of garlic, minced

- A handful of basil, chopped

- ¼ cup chicken broth

- Salt and pepper to taste

- 5 large assorted bell peppers, chopped

Directions:

1. In a medium bowl, combine all ingredients. Place in a Ziploc bag and write the date when the recipe is made. Place inside the freezer.

2. Once you are ready to cook the meal, allow to thaw on the countertop for at least 2 hours. Pour into the crockpot. Close the lid and cook on low for 6 hours or on high for 4 hours.

Nutrition:

Calories: 348

Carbohydrates: 6.8g

Protein: 14.7g

Fat: 28.9g

CHAPTER 2:

Mains

6.   Corned Beef with Cabbage

Preparation time 17 minutes

Cooking time: 9 hours

Servings: 8

Ingredients:

- 4 large carrots

- 1 onion

- Beer

- 1 beef brisket

- 4 cups water

- 10 red potatoes

- 1/2 head cabbage

Directions:

1. Prepare vegetables: peel carrots, cut into matchstick pieces. Quarter the potatoes and slice onion to bite-size pieces. Coarsely chop the cabbage.

2. Grease your cooking dish and place the vegetables over its bottom. Place the beef on top of the vegetables. Pour in beer to cover ingredients and season with spices. Set crock pot and cook for another hour. Serve.

Nutrition:

Calories: 472

Fat: 19g

Carbohydrates: 49g

Protein: 23g

7.   Beef Stroganoff

Preparation time: 11 minutes

Cooking time: 8 hours

Servings: 4

Ingredients:

- Beef stew meat

- Small onion

- 5 tbsp. water

- Worcestershire sauce

- Cream cheese

- 1 can mushroom soup

Directions:

1. Grease crock pot with some butter. Cut the beef into cubes, place evenly over bottom of a cooking bowl. Chop the onion, cover the meat with it.

2. Add some mushroom soup and some Worcestershire sauce. Add the water. Cover with the lid. Cook for 5 hours using a high mode or for 8 hours on low. When the meal is ready, add and stir in cream cheese.

Nutrition:

Calories: 377

Fat: 26g

Carbohydrates: 11g

Protein: 25g

8.   Carnitas

Preparation time: 12 minutes Cooking time: 9-10 hours

Servings: 12

Ingredients:

- 1 boneless pork shoulder

- Salt

- Cumin

- Dried oregano

- Garlic powder

- Ground cinnamon

- Bay leaves

- Chicken broth

Directions:

1. In a small bowl, combine some garlic powder, some salt, dried oregano, cumin, coriander and some cinnamon.

2. Grease your crock pot. Place two bay leaves on the bottom. Place the pork meat to crock pot Pour in the broth.

3. Cook under the lid for about 10 hours on LOW, wait until the meat begins to fall off. Shred with forks before serving.

Nutrition:

Calories: 223

Fat: 13g

Carbohydrates: 1g

Protein: 22g

9.   Hot Potatoes with Pork

Preparation time: 13 minutes Cooking time: 9 hours

Servings: 8

Ingredients:

- 3 carrots

- Chuck roast

- 1 pack dry onion soup mix

- Stalk celery

- 3 large potatoes

- Onion

- 1 cup water

- Species to taste

Directions:

1. Cube the potatoes. Chop carrots, celery, onion. Rub the roast with pepper and salt. Take a large skillet and brown the meat on

other sides. Grease your crock pot with butter or cooking spray, as you like.

2. Place the roast into it and cover with water, soup mix, onion, carrots, celery and potatoes. Cover the lid and leave, cooking, for 8-10 hours with low temperature setting.

Nutrition:

Calories: 540

Fat: 30g

Carbohydrates: 18g

Protein: 45g

CHAPTER 3:

Sides

10.   Thai Side Salad

Preparation time: 15 minutes

Cooking time: 3 Hours

Servings: 8

Ingredients:

- 8 ounces yellow summer squash, peeled and roughly chopped

- 12 ounces zucchini, halved and sliced

- 2 cups button mushrooms, quartered

- 1 red sweet potato, chopped

- 2 leeks, sliced

- 2 tablespoons veggie stock

- 2 garlic cloves, minced

- 2 tablespoon Thai red curry paste

- 1 tablespoon ginger, grated

- 1/3 cup coconut milk

- ¼ cup basil, chopped

Directions:

In your Crock Pot, mix zucchini with summer squash, mushrooms, red pepper, leeks, garlic, stock, curry paste, ginger, coconut milk and basil, toss, cover and cook on Low for 3 hours.

Stir your Thai mix one more time, divide between plates and serve as a side dish.

Nutrition:

Calories 69

Fat 2g

Carbs 8g Protein 2g

11.   Lemon Artichokes

Preparation time: 15 minutes Cooking time: 3 Hours

Servings: 2

Ingredients:

- 1 cup veggie stock

- 2 medium artichokes, trimmed

- 1 tablespoon lemon juice

- 1 tablespoon lemon zest, grated

- Salt to the taste

Directions:

1. In your Crock Pot, mix the artichokes with the stock and the other Ingredients, and then toss it, put the lid on and cook on Low for 3 hours. Divide artichokes between plates and serve as a side dish.

Nutrition: Calories 100 Fat 2g Carbs 10g Protein 4g

12.   Mashed Potatoes

Preparation time: 15 minutes Cooking time: 6 Hours

Servings: 2

Ingredients:

- 1 pound gold potatoes, peeled and cubed

- 2 garlic cloves, chopped

- 1 cup milk

- 1 cup water

- 2 tablespoons butter

- A pinch of salt and white pepper

Directions:

1. In your Crock Pot, mix the potatoes with the water, salt and pepper, put the lid on and cook on Low for 6 hours. Mash the potatoes; add the rest of the Ingredients, whisk and serve.

Nutrition: Calories 135 Fat 4g Carbs 10g Protein 4g

13.   Blueberry Spinach Salad

Preparation time: 15 minutes

Cooking time: 1 Hour

Servings: 3

Ingredients:

- ¼ cup pecans, chopped

- ½ tsp. sugar

- 2 tsp. maple syrup

- 1 tbsp. white vinegar

- 2 tbsp. orange juice

- 1 tbsp. olive oil

- 4 cups spinach

- 2 oranges, peeled and cut into segments

- 1 cup blueberries

Directions:

1. Add pecans, maple syrup, and rest of the fixings to the Crock Pot. Put the crock pot's lid on and set the cooking time to 1 hour on High settings. Serve warm.

Nutrition:

Calories: 140

Fat: 4g

Carbs: 10g

Protein: 3g

14.   Okra and Corn

Preparation time: 15 minutes

Cooking time: 8 Hours

Servings: 4

Ingredients:

- 3 garlic cloves, minced

- 1 small green bell pepper, chopped

- 1 small yellow onion, chopped

- 1 cup water

- 16 ounces okra, sliced

- 2 cups corn

- 1 and ½ teaspoon smoked paprika

- 28 ounces canned tomatoes, crushed

- 1 teaspoon oregano, dried

- 1 teaspoon thyme, dried

- 1 teaspoon marjoram, dried

- A pinch of cayenne pepper

- Salt and black pepper to the taste

Directions:

1. In your Crock Pot, mix garlic with bell pepper, onion, water, okra, corn, paprika, tomatoes, oregano, thyme, marjoram, cayenne, salt and pepper, cover, cook on Low for 8 hours, divide between plates and serve as a side dish.

Nutrition:

Calories 182

Fat 3g

Carbs 8g

Protein 5g

CHAPTER 4:

Seafood

15.   Sea Bass with Fennel and Tomatoes

Preparation time: 15 minutes

Cooking time: 4 hours & 35 minutes

Servings: 11

Ingredients:

For the sea bass:

- 6 oz. fillets of sea bass

- 1 tbsp olive oil

- salt and ground black pepper at will

For tomatoes and fennel:

- 4 bulbs fennel

- 6 Fl oz. extra virgin olive oil

- 1 big can tomatoes

- 1 head garlic

- 5 oz boiling water

- 4 oz. dry white wine

- 2 tbsp chopped fresh oregano leaves

- 2 tbsp balsamic vinegar

- 12 basil leaves

Directions:

1. Wash the fish thoroughly, rinse well. Take off the scales, wipe dry. Take off the skin. Place the pieces in the fridge. Peel the garlic and mince. Wash the fresh leaves of oregano and chop.

2. Remove leaves from fennel. Cut the fennel lengthways into quarters.

3. Heat the oil in a medium-sized saucepan and put the fennel. Cook the fennel turning frequently, for 15 minutes. Fennel must be of brown color.

4. Add the chopped tomatoes, minced garlic, boiling water, wine, oregano and black pepper at will. Let the mixture boil, cover the lid of the saucepan and cook for 20 minutes.

5. Once the ingredients are almost cooked, add balsamic vinegar and basil leaves. Cover with lid again. Take the sea bass from the refrigerator, season with salt and pepper.

6. Open the Crock Pot, spray with cooking spray the bottom and sides of it. Place the sea bass on a bottom of the Crock Pot.

7. Cover the lid and put on high for 4 hours or until the fish is tender when tested with a fork. Remove the fish carefully from the Crock Pot once the cooking time is over and serve on a plate.

8. Place with a spoonful of the tomatoes and fennel into the center of each piece of fish. Enjoy warm!

Nutrition: Calories: 284 arbs: 3g Fat: 13g Protein: 40g

16.   Sea Bass Cuban Style

Preparation time: 15 minutesCooking time: 6 hours & 5 minutes

Servings: 9 Ingredients:

- 2 tsp olive oil 1 ½ cup white onions

- 2 tsp minced garlic

- 4 cups fresh tomatoes

- 1 ½ cups dry white wine

- 1/8 tsp red pepper flakes

- 4 fillets sea bass (6 ounces)

- 2 tsp butter ¼ cup fresh cilantro

- Pepper and salt at will

Directions:

1. Peel the onion and chop. Peel the garlic and mince finely. Wash and chop fresh cilantro. Set aside. Wash the tomatoes, dry with paper towel, take off the seeds, chop them.

2. Heat olive oil in a medium saucepan over high heat. Sautee onions for some time until it gets brown color. Add garlic, and sauté for a minute. Add tomatoes. They must begin to soften.

3. Add wine, toss and add red pepper flakes. Let everything boil a little bit. Add butter. The sauce must thicken.

4. Open the Crock Pot, spray with cooking spray the bottom and sides of it. Place the sea bass fillets on a bottom of the Crock Pot. Pour the sauce over the fillets.

5. Cover the lid and put on low for 6 hours or until the fish is tender when tested with a fork. But check the tenderness of fish fillets from time to time they must not be overcooked.

6. Remove the fish carefully from the Crock Pot once the cooking time is over and serve on a plate together with sauce from the Crock Pot. Serve with fresh dill or cilantro at will.

Nutrition:Calories: 408 Carbs: 17g Fat: 19g Protein: 34g

17. Sticky Asian Sea Bass

Preparation time: 15 minutes

Cooking time: 6 hours

Servings: 9

Ingredients:

- 1 tbsp sesame oil

- ½ red chili

- 3 tbsp sweetener

- 1 tbsp dark soy sauce replaces with tamari

- ¼ tsp ground ginger

- 1 clove garlic

- ¼ Juice of lime

- 2 Sea Bass fillets - skin on

- ½ tsp Almond flour

- fresh coriander torn

- pepper and salt at will

Directions:

1. Peel the garlic and mince finely. Take off the skin of the sea bass fillets. Take a medium-sized bowl, mix the oil, chili, sweetener, soy sauce, ginger, minced garlic.

2. Squeeze the juice of a lime and add to the mixture. Open the Crock Pot, spray with cooking spray the bottom and sides of it.

3. Place the sea bass fillets on a bottom of the Crock Pot. Sprinkle with the flour. Sprinkle with sweet-soy sauce mix.

4. Cover the lid and put on low for 6 hours or until the fish is tender when tested with a fork.

5. Once the cooking time is over, remove the fillets from the Crock Pot on a plate and sprinkle with remained sauce, season with coriander and chili slices.

Nutrition:Calories: 144 Carbs: 22g Fat: 5g Protein: 22g

18.   Crock Pot Fish Fillet

Preparation time: 15 minutes

Cooking time: 4-5 hours

Servings: 5

Ingredients:

- 1 tsp salt, or to taste

- ½ tsp fresh ground black pepper

- 2-3 lb. white fish (cod, sea bass or catfish)

- fresh herbs (mix of parsley, basil, savory, tarragon)

- 2-3 lemons

Directions:

1. Wash and dry with paper towel lemons. Slice thinly. Set aside. Wash the fish thoroughly, rinse well. Take off the scales, wipe dry. Take off the skin.

2. Sprinkle all the sides of the fish with pepper and salt. Open the Crock Pot, spray with cooking spray the bottom and sides of it.

3. Place the fillets on a bottom of the Crock Pot. Place the lemon slices and herbs on top of the fish. Cover the Crock Pot and put on high for 4-5 hours (depending on the fish) until the fish is cooked through fully.

4. Once the cooking time is over, remove the lemon slices and serve the fish fillet with your favorite species. Bon appetite!

Nutrition:

Calories: 72

Carbs: 0g

Fat: 1g

Protein: 16g

19.   Tuna Mornay

Preparation time: 15 minutes

Cooking time: 4 hours & 30 minutes

Servings: 6

Ingredients:

- 1 can condensed cream of celery soup

- 1 can tuna, with brine (with liquid) 425g

- ½ cup sour cream

- 3 shallots

- 1/3 cup water

- Parmesan or cheddar cheese

- salt and pepper at will

Directions:

1. Pell and chop the shallots. Take a medium-sized bowl, join the condensed cream of celery soup, tuna, sour cream, water, shallots. Add also the rest liquid from the tuna.

2. Open the Crock Pot, put all the mixture, cover the lid of the Crock Pot and put on low for 4 hours. Once the cooking time is over, open the lid, add shredded cheese and cover for 30 minutes.

Nutrition:

Calories: 527

Carbs: 57g

Fat: 16g

Protein: 38g

CHAPTER 5:

Poultry

20.   Roasted Chicken with Lemon & Parsley Butter

Preparation time: 5 minutes Cooking Time: 8 hours

Servings: 2 Ingredients:

- 4 lb. chicken, any part 1 whole lemon, sliced

- 2 tbsp butter or ghee

- 1 tbsp parsley, chopped

Directions:

1. Rub chicken all over with salt and pepper to taste. Put it in the
    crockpot and pour 1 cup of water. Cover and cook for 3 hours
    on high.

2. When cooked, add the lemon slices butter and parsley to the crockpot. Cook and cover for another 10 minutes.

Nutrition:

Calories: 300

Fat: 18 g

Carbs: 1 g

Protein: 29 g

21. Onion and Mushroom Chicken Breasts

Preparation time: 5 minutes Cooking Time: 8 hours

Servings: 2 Ingredients:

- 1 sliced onion

- 1 cup sliced mushrooms

- 2 chicken breasts

- 1 cup chicken broth

- Thyme

Directions:

1. Place the half the onion slices on the bottom of the crockpot and add the chicken on top. Top again with the remainder of onion slices.

2. Add all other ingredients carefully into the crockpot. Add salt and pepper to taste. Cook on low for 8 hours.

Nutrition: Calories: 345 Fat: 29 g Carbs: 4 g Protein: 32 g

22. Turkey-Stuffed Peppers

Preparation time: 15 minutes Cooking Time: 8 hours

Servings: 2 Ingredients:

- 1/2 lb. turkey, ground

- 2 whole green bell peppers, top cut off and insides scraped off

- 12 oz jar tomato sauce

Directions:

1. Mix turkey, 1 tbsp tomato sauce and onion and garlic to taste in a bowl. Separate mixture into two parts and put them inside the peppers.

2. Place the stuffed peppers in the crockpot and add the remaining tomato sauce. Add 1/4 cup of water. Cover and cook for 8 hours on low.

Nutrition: Calories: 422 Fat: 27.5 g Carbs: 3.6 g Protein: 30.8 g

23. Greek Chicken

Preparation time: 5 minutes Cooking Time: 6 hours

Servings: 2 Ingredients:

- 2 chicken breasts, skinless

- 1 1/2 tbsp Greek Rub

- 1 1/2 tbsp lemon juice

- 1 chicken bouillon cube dissolved in water

Directions:

1. Coat each breast with Greek Rub, then rub with garlic powder. Put the chicken breasts in the crockpot and spray with lemon juice.

2. Pour the chicken bouillon mixture in the crockpot. Cook for 6 hours on low.

Nutrition: Calories: 369 Fat: 29.8 g Carbs: 4 g Protein: 28.7 g

24. Creamy Mexican Chicken

Preparation time: 5 minutes

Cooking Time: 6 hours

Servings: 2

Ingredients:

- 1/3 cup sour cream

- 1/4 cup chicken stock

- 7 oz diced tomatoes

- 1/2 pack taco seasoning

- 1 lb. chicken breast

Directions:

1. In the crockpot, mix all ingredients until well combined. Cover and cook for 6 hours on low.

Nutrition: Calories: 262 Fat: 13 g Carbs: 5.8 g Protein: 32 g

CHAPTER 6:

Meat

25.   Onion and Bison Soup

Preparation time: 15 minutes

Cooking time: 6 hours

Servings: 8

Ingredients:

- 1 tablespoon olive oil

- 6 onions, sliced

- 2 pounds bison roast

- 4 cups beef stock

- ½ cup sherry

- 3 sprigs of thyme

- 1 bay leaf

- salt and pepper to taste

Directions:

1. Set the cooking on high and add the olive oil. Sauté the onions until brown. Add the rest of the ingredients and close the lid. Set the cooking time on low and cook for 6 hours

Nutrition:

Calories: 212

Carbohydrates: 4.3g

Protein: 25.78g

Fat: 10.34g

26. **Pepper Beef Tongue Stew**

Preparation time: 15 minutes

Cooking time: 8 hours

Servings: 10

Ingredients:

- 3 pounds sliced beef tongue, boiled and cleaned

- 1 onion, chopped

- 6 cloves of garlic, minced

- 1 red bell pepper, diced

- 1 yellow bell pepper, diced

- 2 cups chicken stock

- 8-ounce can of tomato sauce

- 2 jalapeno peppers, diced

- salt and pepper to taste

- 1 teaspoon Cajun spice

- 1 ¾ stick of butter

- 1 bunch of green onion, chopped

Directions:

1. Place the beef tongue, onion, garlic, and bell peppers in the crockpot. Add the chicken stock and tomato sauce. Stir in the jalapeno pepper and season with salt, pepper and Cajun spice.

2. Cook on low temperature for 8 hours. Once cooked, add butter and garnish with green onions.

Nutrition:

Calories: 441

Carbohydrates: 9.39g

Protein: 28.57g

Fat: 31.07g

27.   Mexican Beef Chili

Preparation time: 10 minutes

Cooking time: 8 hours

Servings: 8

Ingredients:

- 1 onion, chopped

- 2 cloves of garlic, minced

- 4 stalks of celery, chopped

- 2-pound ground beef

- 8 ounces of canned tomatoes

- 1 cup fresh tomatoes, diced

- 2 tablespoon chili powder

- 1 tablespoon cumin

- 2 teaspoons smoked paprika

- salt and pepper to taste

- a dash of smoked paprika

Directions:

1. Place the onions, garlic and celery at the bottom of the crockpot. Add the ground beef and make sure that the meat is crumbled.

2. Pour in the canned tomatoes and fresh tomatoes. Add the rest of the spices and seasonings. Cook on low for 8 hours or on high for 6 hours.

Nutrition:

Calories: 316

Carbohydrates: 5.66g

Protein: 29.88g

Fat: 19.01g

28.   **Ground Beef Minestrone Soup**

Preparation time: 15 minutes

Cooking time: 8 hours

Servings: 8

Ingredients:

- 1 pound ground beef

- 1 onion, diced

- 1 tablespoon garlic, minced

- 3 cups of water

- 2 small zucchinis, diced

- 1 stalk celery, diced

- ½ cup vegetable broth

- 1 can diced tomatoes

- ½ teaspoon basil

- ½ teaspoon dried oregano

Directions:

1. Set the crockpot on high and add the ground beef. Stir in the onion and garlic and sauté for 3 minutes or until meat is slightly browned.

2. Add water and the rest of the ingredients. Adjust the temperature and cook on low for 8 hours.

Nutrition:

Calories: 157

Carbohydrates: 2.86g

Protein: 14.38g

Fat:9.27g

29.   Bacon, Chuck Roast and Cabbage Stew

Preparation time: 15 minutes Cooking time: 7 hours

Servings: 8 Ingredients:

- ½ pound uncured bacon strips

- 2 onions, sliced

- 1 clove of garlic, crushed

- 3 pounds chuck roast cut into 2-inch thick pieces

- 1 small cabbage, sliced

- 1 sprig of thyme

- 1 cup beef bone broth

- salt and pepper to taste

Directions:

1. Place the bacon slices in the bottom of the crockpot. Add the onion and garlic. Pour in the chuck roast on top followed by the cabbage slices.

2. Add the thyme and broth. Season with salt and pepper. Cook on low for 7 hours.

Nutrition:

Calories: 309

Carbohydrates: 8.9g

Protein: 35.88g

Fat: 14.77g

30. Lemon Beef

Preparation time: 15 minutes

Cooking Time: 5 Hours

Servings: 4

Ingredients:

- 1-pound beef sirloin, chopped

- 3 tablespoons lemon juice

- 1 teaspoon curry powder

- 1 teaspoon chili flakes

- 1 teaspoon lemon zest, grated

- ½ teaspoon salt

- 1 tablespoon keto tomato sauce

- 1 teaspoon butter

- ½ cup of water

- ½ teaspoon cayenne pepper

Directions:

1. In the crockpot, mix the beef with lemon juice and zest and the other ingredients and toss. Close the lid and cook beef sirloin for 5 hours on High. Divide between plates and serve.

Nutrition:

Calories 229

Fat 8.7g

Carbs 1.2g

Protein 34.5g

31.   Caraway Ribs

Preparation time: 15 minutes

Cooking Time: 4.5 Hours

Servings: 4

Ingredients:

- 15 oz pork spare ribs

- 1 ½ teaspoons caraway seeds

- ½ teaspoon cumin, ground

- ½ teaspoon sweet paprika

- ½ teaspoon garam masala

- ½ teaspoon dried oregano

- ½ teaspoon dried basil

- 1 tablespoon olive oil

- 1/3 cup water

Directions:

1. In your crockpot, mix the ribs with caraway seeds and the other ingredients. Close the lid. Cook the spare ribs for 4.5 hours on High.

Nutrition:

Calories 311

Fat 15g

Carbs 7.3g

Protein 20.1g

32.   Dinner Lamb Shanks

Preparation time: 15 minutesCooking Time: 8 Hours

Servings: 3 Ingredients:

- 1 tablespoon of olive oil 3/4 cup of bone broth

- ½ teaspoon of rosemary, dried, crushed

- 1 tablespoon of melted butter 3 whole garlic cloves, peeled

- Salt and black pepper, to taste

- 3/4 tablespoon of Sugar-free tomato paste

- 1 ¼ tablespoon of fresh lemon juice

Directions:

1. Start by putting all the fixings into your Crockpot. Cover its lid and cook for 8 hours on Low settings. Once done, remove its lid and mix well. Garnish as desired. Serve warm.

Nutrition: Calories 188 Fat 12.5 g Carbs 4.9 g Protein 14.6 g

CHAPTER 7:

Vegetables

33.   Eggplant Salad

Preparation time: 15 minutes

Cooking time: 7-8 hours

Servings: 6

Ingredients:

- 1 red onion, peeled and sliced

- 2 red bell peppers, de-seeded and sliced

- 1 eggplant, quartered and sliced

- 1 can chopped tomatoes

- 1 tablespoon smoked paprika

Directions:

1. Grease a 4-quart crock pot with a non-stick cooking spray, and place all of the ingredients inside. Season with salt and ground black pepper and stir until all ingredients are well-combined.

2. Cover and seal the crock pot with its lid, and adjust the cooking timer for 7 to 8 hours, allowing it to cook on a low heat setting. Serve with cooked cauliflower rice.

Nutrition:

Calories: 130

Carbohydrates: 8.9 g

Fats: 9.4 g

Protein: 2.1 g

34.   Cauliflower and Cheese

Preparation time: 15 minutes

Cooking time: 2 hours & 30 minutes

Servings: 6

Ingredients:

- 1 large cauliflower head, split into florets

- 1/4 teaspoon garlic powder

- 3 tablespoons melted butter

- 1 cup shredded cheddar cheese

- 4 oz sour cream

Directions:

1. Grease a 4-quart crock pot, place the cauliflower florets inside, and season with salt and black pepper.

2. Seal the crock pot with its lid, and adjust the cooking timer for 2 1/2 hours, allowing to cook at a low heat setting.

3. Stir the remaining ingredients together, then pour over the cauliflower florets. Allow to continue to cook for a further hour. Serve immediately.

Nutrition:

Calories: 199

Carbohydrates: 5 g

Fats: 17 g

Protein: 8 g

35.　Thai Yellow Curry

Preparation time: 15 minutes

Cooking time: 8 hours

Servings: 6

Ingredients:

- 2 teaspoons minced garlic and 1 tablespoon grated ginger

- 1/2 cup cherry tomatoes, halved

- 2 teaspoons Thai yellow curry paste

- 2 teaspoons fish sauce and 3 teaspoons soy sauce

- 1 can full-fat coconut milk, unsweetened

Directions:

1. In a 4-quart crock pot, place all the ingredients apart from the tomatoes. Stir until mixed, then seal the crock pot with its lid.

2. Set the cooking timer for 7 hours and allow to cook at a low heat setting. Add the tomatoes to the mixture, and allow to cook

for a further hour. Garnish with cilantro, and serve with cauliflower rice.

Nutrition:

Calorie: 185

Carbohydrates: 9 g

Fats: 29 g

Protein: 9.4 g

36. Vegetable Curry

Preparation time: 15 minutes

Cooking time: 4 hours

Servings: 5

Ingredients:

- 1 cup cauliflower florets

- 2 medium-sized sweet potatoes, peeled and cubed

- 3 tablespoons red curry paste

- 3 tablespoons soy sauce and 2 teaspoon Sriracha sauce

- 1 can full-fat coconut milk, unsweetened

Directions:

1. Place the cauliflower florets and sweet potatoes in a 4-quart crock pot. Mix the remaining ingredients together in a separate bowl, and season with a pinch of salt and a tablespoon of brown sugar.

2. Pour this mixture over the vegetables, then seal the crock pot with its lid. Set the cooking timer for 4 hours, and allow to cook at a low heat setting. Garnish with cilantro and basil and serve with cauliflower rice.

Nutrition:

Calories: 205

Carbohydrates: 12 g

Fats: 13.5 g

Protein: 9 g

CHAPTER 8:

Soups & Stews

37.   Shrimp Soup

Preparation Time: 15 minutes

Cooking Time: 5 hours

Servings: 6

Ingredients:

- 1 onion, chopped

- ½ of green bell pepper, seeded and chopped

- 1 (14½-oz.) can diced tomatoes with juice

- 2½ oz. canned mushrooms

- ¼ cup black olives, pitted and sliced

- 2 garlic cloves, minced

- 1 (8-oz.) can tomato sauce

- 2 bay leaves

- 1 tsp. dried basil

- ¼ tsp. fennel seed, crushed

- Salt and freshly ground black pepper, to taste

- ½ cup dry white wine

- ½ cup orange juice

- 2 (14-oz.) cans chicken broth

- 2 lb. medium shrimp, peeled and deveined

Directions:

1. In a crock pot, place all the ingredients except for shrimp and stir to combine. Set the crock pot on "Low" and cook, covered for about 4-4½ hours.

2. Uncover the crock pot and stir in the shrimp. Set the crock pot on "Low" and cook, covered for about 20-30 minutes. Uncover the crock pot and discard the bay leaves. Serve hot.

Nutrition:

Calories: 234

Carbohydrates: 11.5g

Protein: 37.1g

Fat: 3.5g

38. Detox Vegetarian Soup

Preparation Time: 20 minutes

Cooking Time: 6 hours

Servings: 8

Ingredients:

- 1 cup green lentils

- ¾ cup yellow split peas

- 2 cups butternut squash, peeled and cubed

- 2 cups potatoes, chopped

- 2 cups carrots, peeled and sliced

- 2 cups celery stalks, chopped

- 1 onion, chopped

- 5 garlic cloves, minced

- 8-10 cups vegetable broth

- 2 tsp. Herbes de Provence

- Salt, to taste

- ½ cup olive oil

- 2-3 cups fresh kale, tough ribs removed and chopped

- 1 cup fresh parsley, chopped

Directions:

1. In a crock pot, place all the ingredients except for oil, kale and parsley and stir to combine. Set the crock pot on "High" and cook, covered for about 5-6 hours.

2. Uncover the crock pot and transfer about 4 cups of soup in a bowl. Set aside to cool for about 2-3 minutes.

3. Meanwhile, in the remaining soup, add the kale and parsley and stir until wilted. In a blender, add the cooled soup and oil and pulse until slightly smooth.

4. Return the pureed soup into the crock pot with the remaining soup and stir to combine. Serve immediately.

Nutrition: Calories: 370 Carbohydrates: 44g Protein: 17.9g Fat: 14.6g

39.   Aromatic Veggie Soup

Preparation Time: 20 minutes

Cooking Time: 4 hours

Servings: 8

Ingredients:

- 2 russet potatoes, scrubbed and cut into ¼-inch thick rounds

- 2 large carrots, peeled and sliced into rounds

- 1½ lb. green cabbage, cored and chopped

- 2 medium onions, sliced into half

- 2 garlic cloves, minced

- 1 tbsp. ground cumin

- 1 tsp. sweet Spanish paprika

- ½ tsp. ground coriander

- ¼ tsp. ground turmeric

- 1 bay leaf

- Salt and freshly ground black pepper, to taste

- 1 cup tomato sauce

- 3 tbsp. extra-virgin olive oil

- 7 cups low-sodium vegetable broth

- ½ cups fresh dill

- 2 tbsp. fresh lemon juice

Directions:

1. In a crock pot, place all the ingredients except for dill and lemon juice and stir to combine. Set the crock pot on "High" and cook, covered for about 4 hours.

2. Uncover the crock pot and stir in the dill and lemon juice. Serve hot.

Nutrition:

Calories: 155

Carbohydrates: 22.6g

Protein: 5.4g Fat: 5.8g

40.   Minestrone Soup

Preparation Time: 20 minutes

Cooking Time: 8 ½ hours

Servings: 12

Ingredients:

- 2 medium potatoes, peeled and chopped

- 2 medium carrots, peeled and chopped

- 2 celery stalks, chopped

- 1 (14½ oz.) can diced tomatoes with juice

- 1 medium onion, chopped

- 3 garlic cloves, minced

- 2 bay leaves

- 1 tbsp. Italian seasoning

- Salt and freshly ground black pepper, to taste

- 1 (32-oz.) carton vegetable broth

- 3 cups tomato juice

- 2 cups water

- 1 small zucchini, chopped

- 1 (16-oz.) can kidney beans, rinsed and drained

- 1 (15-oz.) can cannellini beans, rinsed and drained

- 1 (14½-oz.) can cut green beans, drained

- 1 cup uncooked ditalini pasta

- 1 cup Parmesan cheese, shredded

Directions:

1. In a crock pot, place the potatoes, carrots, celery, tomatoes with juice, onion, garlic, bay leaves, Italian seasoning, salt, black pepper, broth, tomato juice and water and stir to combine.

2. Set the crock pot on "Low" and cook, covered for about 6-8 hours. Uncover the crock pot and stir in the remaining ingredients except for cheese.

3. Set the crock pot on "High" and cook, covered for about 30 minutes. Uncover the crock pot and discard bay leaves. Serve hot with the topping of Parmesan cheese.

Nutrition:

Calories: 370

Carbohydrates: 62.4g

Protein: 23.7g

Fat: 4.1g

41.   Filling Vegetarian Soup

Preparation Time: 15 minutes

Cooking Time: 3½ hours

Servings: 6

Ingredients:

- 3 (14 -oz.) cans vegetable broth

- 1 (15-oz.) can tomato puree

- 1 (15-oz.) can white beans, rinsed and drained

- ½ cup converted white rice

- ½ cup onion, chopped finely

- 2 garlic cloves, minced

- 1 tsp. dried basil, crushed

- Salt and freshly ground black pepper, to taste

- 8 cups fresh spinach, chopped

- ¼ cup Parmesan cheese, shredded

Directions:

1. In a crock pot, place all the ingredients except for spinach and cheese and stir to combine. Set the crock pot on "High" and cook, covered for about 2½-3½ hours.

2. Uncover the crock pot and stir in the spinach until wilted. Serve hot with the topping of Parmesan cheese.

Nutrition:

Calories: 379

Carbohydrates: 64.9g

Protein: 25.4g

Fat: 3.1g

CHAPTER 9:

Snacks

42.   Parmesan Green Beans

Preparation Time: 10 minutes Cooking Time: 3 hours

Servings: 2 Ingredients:

- 2 oz. Parmesan, grated

- 5 oz. green beans

- ¼ cup almond milk, unsweetened

- 1 teaspoon paprika

Directions:

1. Place the green beans in the crock pot. Add almond milk and

    paprika. Stir and cook the green beans for 2 hours on High.

2. Sprinkle the green beans with Parmesan cheese and cook for 1 hour more on High. Chill the cooked green beans slightly and serve!

Nutrition:

Calories 185

Fat 13.5g

Carbs 8.3g

Protein 11.2g

43.   Zucchini Fries

Preparation Time: 15 minutes

Cooking Time: 2 hours

Servings: 4

Ingredients:

- 1 zucchini

- ¼ cup almond flour

- 1 egg

- 1 tablespoon butter

- ½ cup almond flour

- 1 teaspoon onion powder

Directions:

1. Wash the zucchini well and cut into sticks. Beat the egg in a bowl. Dip the zucchini sticks in the whisked egg then sprinkle the zucchini sticks with the onion powder and dip them in the almond flour.

2. Transfer the zucchini sticks into the crock pot. Add butter and cook the zucchini for 2 hours on High. Serve the cooked zucchini fries immediately!

Nutrition:

Calories 61

Fat 5g

Carbs 2.6g

Protein 2.4g

44.   Cauliflower Fritters

Preparation Time: 15 minutes

Cooking Time: 2 hours & 30 minutes

Servings: 6

Ingredients:

- 8 oz cauliflower

- 1 egg

- 2 tablespoons almond flour

- 1 tablespoon butter

- 1 teaspoon dried oregano

Directions:

1. Chop the cauliflower roughly and place them in a blender. Blend the cauliflower until smooth and transfer into a mixing bowl.

2. Add the almond flour and dried oregano. Add the beaten egg and stir it well. Make into medium fritters.

3. Place the butter in the crock pot and add the fritters. Cook the cauliflower fritters for 2.5 hours on High. Serve the meal!

Nutrition:

Calories 91

Fat 7.4g

Carbs 4.2g

Protein 3.7g

45.   Zucchini Latkes

Preparation Time: 15 minutes Cooking Time: 2 hours

Servings: 3 Ingredients:

- 1 zucchini, grated

- 1 onion, grated

- 1 teaspoon butter

- 1 tablespoon almond flour

- 1 teaspoon salt

Directions:

1. Mix grated zucchini, onion, and salt. Add almond flour and stir the mixture until smooth. Add the butter to the crock pot.

2. Make the medium latkes using 2 spoons. Place them in the crock pot and close the lid. Cook the zucchini latkes for 2 hours on High. Transfer the latkes to a platter and serve!

Nutrition: Calories 90 Fat 6.1g Carbs 7.6g Protein 3.2g

46. Zucchini Tots with Cheese

Preparation Time: 15 minutes Cooking Time: 3 hours

Servings: 6

Ingredients:

- 1 zucchini, grated

- 3 oz. Parmesan, grated

- 1 teaspoon dried dill

- 1 teaspoon dried oregano

- ½ teaspoon salt

- 1 egg

- 1 tablespoon almond flour

- 1 tablespoon butter

Directions:

1. Mix the zucchini, Parmesan, dried dill, dried oregano, salt, almond flour, and beaten egg. Stir the mixture until smooth.

2. Form small tots and place them in the crock pot. The mixture should not be liquid so add more almond flour if needed in order to form the tots.

3. Add butter to the crock pot and close the lid. Cook the zucchini tots for 3 hours on High. Chill the zucchini tots to room temperature and serve!

Nutrition:

Calories 106

Fat 8.1g

Carbs 2.9g

Protein 7g

CHAPTER 10:

Desserts

47. Pineapple Upside Down Cake

Preparation time: 15 minutes

Cooking time: 5 hours

Servings: 10

Ingredients:

- 1 cup butter, softened

- 1/2 cup light brown sugar

- 1/2 cup white sugar

- 2 eggs

- 1 cup all-purpose flour

- 1/2 cup ground almonds

- 1 teaspoon baking powder

- 1/4 teaspoon salt

- 1/2 teaspoon cinnamon powder

- 2 tablespoons butter to grease the pot

- 1 can pineapple chunks, drained

Directions:

1. Grease the pot with butter then place the pineapple chunks in the pot. For the cake, mix the softened butter, brown sugar and white sugar in a bowl.

2. Add the eggs, one by one, mixing well after each addition. Fold in the flour, almonds, baking powder and salt, as well as cinnamon.Pour the batter over the pineapple and bake for 5 hours on low settings.

Nutrition: Calories: 360 Carbs: 53g Fat: 16g Protein: 2g

48.   Pure Berry Crumble

Preparation time: 15 minutes

Cooking time: 5 hours

Servings: 8

Ingredients:

- 1 pound fresh mixed berries

- 1 tablespoon cornstarch

- 1/4 cup white sugar

- 1 teaspoon lemon zest

- 1 cup all-purpose flour

- 1/4 cup cornstarch

- 1 pinch salt

- 1/2 teaspoon baking powder

- 1/2 cup butter, chilled and cubed

- 2 tablespoons sugar

Directions:

1. Mix the berries, cornstarch, 1/4 cup sugar and lemon zest in your crock pot. For the topping, combine the flour, cornstarch, salt and baking powder in a bowl.

2. Add the butter and mix well until the mixture is grainy. Spread the mixture over the berries and cook on low settings for 5 hours. Serve the crumble chilled.

Nutrition:

Calories: 195

Carbs: 20g

Fat: 12g

Protein: 2g

49.   Apple Sour Cream Crostata

Preparation time: 15 minutes

Cooking time: 6 hours

Servings: 8

Ingredients:

- 2 pounds Granny Smith apples, peeled, cored and sliced

- 1 tablespoon cornstarch

- 1 teaspoon cinnamon powder

- 1/4 cup light brown sugar

- 1 1/2 cups all-purpose flour

- 1/2 cup butter, chilled and cubed

- 1 pinch salt

- 2 tablespoons white sugar

- 1/2 cup sour cream

Directions:

1. Mix the butter, flour, salt and white sugar in a bowl. Rub the mix well with your fingertips until grainy then stir in the sour cream and knead for a few times.

2. Roll the dough on a floured working surface to match the size of your crock pot. Transfer the dough in your crock pot.

3. For the topping, mix the apples, cornstarch, cinnamon and light brown sugar in a bowl. Place the mix over the dough.

4. Cover the pot and cook on low settings for 6 hours. Serve the crostata chilled.

Nutrition:

Calories: 240

Carbs: 36g

Fat: 11g

Protein: 3g

50.   **Autumnal Bread Pudding**

Preparation time: 15 minutes

Cooking time: 5 hours

Servings: 8

Ingredients:

- 16 oz. bread cubes

- 2 red apples, peeled and diced

- 2 pears, peeled and diced

- 1/2 cup golden raisins

- 1/4 cup butter, melted

- 2 cups whole milk

- 4 eggs, beaten

- 1/2 cup white sugar

- 1 teaspoon vanilla extract

- 1/2 teaspoon cinnamon powder

Directions:

1. Mix the bread cubes, apples, pears and raisins in your crock pot. Combine the butter, milk, eggs, sugar, vanilla and cinnamon in a bowl. Pour this mixture over the bread.

2. Cover the pot and cook on low settings for 5 hours. Serve the bread pudding slightly warm.

Nutrition:

Calories: 287

Carbs: 39g

Fat: 12g

Protein: 7g

Conclusion

You have to the end of this amazing cookbook, but always remember that this is not the end of your cooking journey with the crockpot; but instead, this is your stepping stone towards more cooking glory. We hope you have found your favorite recipes that are time-saving and money-saving.

Now that you know how Crockpot works and the many benefits of using it, maybe it is time for you to buy one for your family, in case you haven't owned one. When it comes to time spent preparing meals for your family, Crock-Pot is a lifesaver. If you are a busy person, a powerful solution is to use the crockpot.

You will also love to own one if you want to make your life simpler at work if you want to make your life simpler at home, and if you want to preserve some of the natural resources. You could also use one if you want to lean towards a healthier lifestyle as cooking in the crockpot is conducive to health than in the oven.

The crockpot can be used in making homemade and custom-made buffets, even in catering services. You can use it for cooking for your staff for special occasions and for showing them how to cook a tasty and healthier dish for your guests well within their own crockpot.

After choosing the best one for you, maybe it is time for you to know more about the recipes you should use. There are various recipes in this cookbook that are perfect for crockpot cooking, and they will definitely be useful and beneficial for you.

Moreover, whether you are a newbie or an experienced cook, you are going to love this cookbook as it is packed with every conceivable taste. You have discovered more than 1000 recipes in this cookbook that you can put into practice using your crockpot. You can always customize the recipes to suit your taste buds, as you can make any recipe mild or hot, sweet or sour; you have all the freedom to make the recipes your own. The best thing about cooking using a crockpot is that you just need to add the main ingredients, and no other complicated cooking preparation is needed; the crockpot will add most of the other ingredients for you.

This crockpot cookbook covered all the recipes that are sure to make your heart happy and your taste buds happy as well. These meals are not just easy to make, but they will also save you hours of preparation and cleanup. The crockpot is also famous for its great nutritional value. It is the best nutritional value you will ever get. The high levels of healthy fats, proteins, and fiber you get when you cook using the crockpot are entirely natural, which everybody needs. Some of the ingredients are healthy enough to be consumed on their own.

When you are done with the crockpot recipes, just store them and access them whenever you need to. You could use them for a party, and your guests will love the recipes. They will love your attention to detail and your hospitality. You can invite them over, and when they are all set to leave, you will say that you must give them something of yours that you hope they will like, and now you know what recipes to include in such a thought that they will love and appreciate.

The only limit of the crockpot is your imagination and creativity. That is definitely why you fell in love with the crockpot. That is why you are going to expand your love for the crockpot through all these recipes.

After cooking with these recipes, you are sure that there are so many advantages of cooking with the crockpot. With all that said, use these recipes, and you will see that cooking is much easier than you have ever imagined it and that cooking can be fun as well. Go ahead and put your own signature twist on these recipes and let these recipes add magic to your life.

CPSIA information can be obtained
at www.ICGtesting.com
Printed in the USA
BVHW091950220421
605649BV00006B/127